Isaiah Has the Bedtime Blues

story by
Tracey Reed

illustrated by
Greg K. Reed

AuthorHouse™
1663 Liberty Drive
Bloomington, IN 47403
www.authorhouse.com
Phone: 833-262-8899

Because of the dynamic nature of the Internet, any web addresses or links contained in this book may have changed since publication and may no longer be valid. The views expressed in this work are solely those of the author and do not necessarily reflect the views of the publisher, and the publisher hereby disclaims any responsibility for them.

Any people depicted in stock imagery provided by Getty Images are models, and such images are being used for illustrative purposes only. Certain stock imagery © Getty Images.

This book is printed on acid-free paper.

ISBN: 978-1-4389-4886-7 (sc)

Print information available on the last page.

Published by AuthorHouse 09/22/2021

authorHOUSE®

"...I'll eat my green beans!"

Da-Dunnaaa-Da--Duh

"...I'll clean up my room..."

Da- Dunnaaa-Da-Duh

"...I'll even vacuum..."

Da-Dunnaaa-Da-Duh

"…I'll even take a bath…"

Da-Dunnaaa-Da-Duh

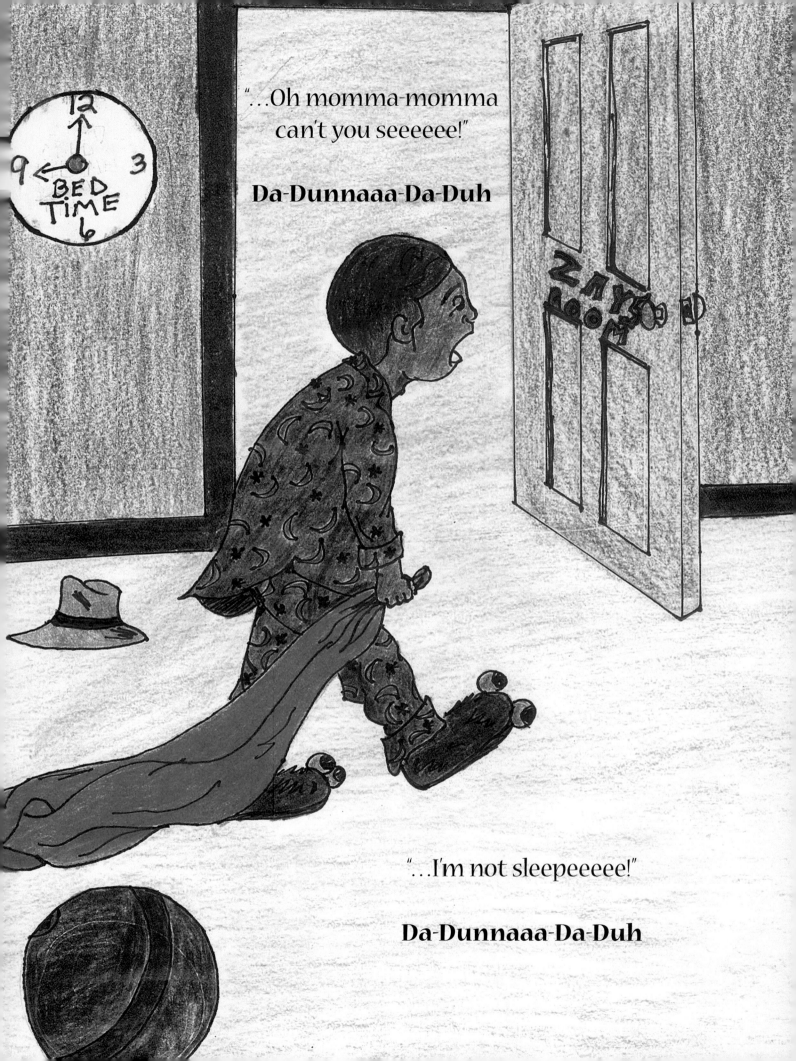

"...Oh momma-momma pleeeeeease!"
Da-Dunnaaa-Da-Duh
"...I'm down on my knees..."
Da-Dunnaaa-Da-Duh
"...and beggin' you please!"
Da-Dunnaaa-Da-Duh

"…Oh momma what must I do??"
Da- Dunnaaa-Da-Duh
"…To stay up late with you??"
Da-Dunnaaa-Da-Duh

"…I'll sit quietly in bed…"

Da-Dunnaaa-Da-Duh

"…I'll even rest my head!"

Da-Dunnaaa-Da-Duh

"...I'll give up my bike...if only for this one night..."

Da Dunnaaaaa...

...ZZZZZzzzzzzzzzzzzzzz...

THE END

Printed in the United States
by Baker & Taylor Publisher Services